AF469069

The Southern Scene

THE SOUTHERN SCENE

An Album of photographs by
Maurice W. Earley

Oxford Publishing Co . Oxford

First Published 1973
SBN 0 902888 19 6

Halftones
By Oxford Lithoplates Ltd.

Printed in the City of Oxford

Published by
Oxford Publishing Co.
5 Lewis Close
Risinghurst
Oxford.

Preface

The railway enthusiast living in Reading was a very lucky man, especially in the pre-1923 days when no less than three railways served the town. The Great Western was naturally the 'giant', but both the L.S.W.R. and the S.E.C.R. added their quota of interest. The L.S.W.R. came in via Basingstoke to the Great Western station, passing through Reading West station with the cross-country trains. There was also the S.E.C.R. from Redhill running into their own station (alongside the Great Western) called "Reading South" but now demolished. The L.S.W.R. trains from Waterloo also used the S.E.C.R. line from Wokingham Junction to Reading by virtue of "running powers". This created the unusual situation whereby the L.S.W.R. came into Reading from opposite directions but not into the same stations, and therefore never actually met in the course of their duties. The Waterloo line trains were monopolised by the famous M.7, 0—4—4T engines, although up to the first World War and even in 1915, one could occasionally see an Adams "Radial" 4—4—2T on such trains. On the local trains from Basingstoke (which were worked by the L.S.W.R.) one could usually see only the Adams 4—4—0's and the "Jubilee" 0—4—2's, but these duties were shared with the Great Western as well. Added to all this were the S.E.C.R. services on the Reading to Redhill branch (during the period mentioned) in the hands of the rebuilds of Stirling's F and B classes of 4—4—0's.

From the old house I spent many hours with a telescope watching both the Great Western and the trains over the S.E.C.R. line. I can still see the various liveries such as S.E.C.R. reddish, or dark maroon of the coaches, the salmon upper panels and brown lower of the L.S.W.R. stock, and finally the Great Western crimson lake adopted after 1912. All three companies painted their engines in different shades of green, which was quite a colourful sight as can be appreciated, and perhaps it was this scene on its own which roused my interest in the Constituents of the Southern Railway. Then again it was the annual holidays when my parents seemed always to choose resorts served either by the L.S.W.R. or the S.E.C.R., such as Brighton, Margate, Isle of Wight or Folkestone, except for the holiday in 1916 when we went to Weston-Super-Mare. I cannot recall the Great Western being used on such occasions before 1923. My father's business ran an annual day's outing by a Special train, again to the South Coast resorts, and I can still see one of these trains standing in the S.E.C.R. station at Reading with its "bird-cage" stock, all beautifully clean inside and out, but where we went on that day I have completely forgotten! It was the Brighton holidays of 1911 and 1912, and the next two to Folkestone which it will be hard to forget. The sight of the famous "Southern Belle" arriving at Brighton "dead on the dot" at 12 noon with a beautiful train of 12 wheeled Pullmans really made a deep impression.

On the Folkestone holidays of 1913 and 1914 it was the Harbour branch which left its mark. Our guest house looked straight at the Harbour station, and I fancy my parents made a point of securing a table in the window at meal times, so that I could see the trains leaving with THREE class "R" of "R.1" 0–6–0T's hard at work. Naturally I had to return there in 1952 plus the camera to record such a scene, but on that occasion they were using FOUR of these engines on the trains! One day in 1913 whilst at Folkestone my brother took me up to the Junction station to see the boat trains leaving the reversing sidings there for London, and I shall certainly never forget the sound and sight of the "D" class S.E.C.R. 4–4–0 starting up with a full load of nearly 300 tons regulator wide open and I should imagine 75% cut-off, whistle blowing (the station had staggered platforms) and everybody standing well clear – could one ever forget such a scene?!

At odd periods from 1919 to 1921 I had to regularly travel to Basingstoke on business, so then the delights of the L.S.W.R. main-line were savoured. With the wide expanse of the Hampshire scenery many pleasant photographic spots were duly noted for when I possessed a camera. In those days it was a matter of the Urie 4–6–0's, with 4–4–0's of all classes, many of which had been rebuilt with Urie superheaters, and in addition those weird Drummond 4–2–2–0's hovering around with various classes of tank engines to complete the scene, but it is still the familiar screech of the L.S.W.R. whistle and the curious "buzzing" sound of the safety valves which persist in my memory.

Readers will have to forgive the many shots taken at two locations, one of which is Earley station, and the other at the well-known junction at Battledown (usually known as Worting). In the former case the spot was within very easy walking distance from home, and there was a very convenient public crossing just south of the station with a backcloth of trees. There was a typical S.E.C.R. bracket signal to complete the scene, and with most trains calling at the station, it was all a photographer could ask for! Battledown (or shall we say Worting) was further afield and needed some form of transport of one's own to reach, but was still only about 15 miles' distance. It had a lovely parking space right beside the line with the wide expanse of open farmland all around, together with that attractive fly-over bridge as a kind of background, or an excellent frame for trains coming under it on a curve. What more could one want?!

Lastly we must not forget that both the L.S.W.R. and the S.E.C.R. were prone to regard their train services on both the Basingstoke and Redhill routes to Reading as a kind of "last ditch" for their older locomotives which was a boon to the railway photographer. In this connection one must recall the hard work put in for many long years by the S.E.C.R. rebuilds of the Stirling F. and F.1 classes of 4–4–0's with trains usually stopping at all stations on a heavily graded line and with 7′ diam. coupled-wheels into the bargain. One might say that having "lived" with these die-hards it was quite a shock to see what appeared to be an immense smoke-box glaring at me in the

Reading (S.R.) Sheds in 1948, photograph taken from the East Main Box entrance of the G.W.R. It will be noted that two S.E.C.R. F.1.4–4–0's, two N. class 2–6–0's and an ex L.S.W.R. G.6 0–6–0T are visible in this scene. The Goods Sheds in the background are on site of the original station built on the opening of the branch in 1849 according to a contemporary painting.

form of a Borsig "L" class 4–4–0 at Ashford station on the memorable 4th August 1914, when on our way home from the annual holiday at Folkestone. Perhaps it was that and the very familiar Stirling rebuilds around Reading that gave me a sneaking love for the S.E.C.R., plus the evergreen "bird-cage" sets mostly used on the local trains – may the memory of that line linger on for ever not forgetting that "D" class 4–4–0 of the S.E.C.R. starting up at Folkestone Junction. Then there were the war years from 1914 to 1918 when with a school chum we spent many hours in Palmer Park recording all we saw on the Reading-Redhill route of the S.E.C.R., the details of which form another story, but unfortunately in my pre-camera days. In two World Wars that stretch of line, with the L.S.W.R. Reading-Basingstoke branch, have borne a great part in our Island's history.

So reader are you surprised now that I took so many photographs on the Southern – surely not?

Lastly, but not least, the Southern did not display any haste to condemn the older engines of the Constituent Companies when Grouping came so the photographer had a wide variety of types and classes available even right up to the days of Nationalisation – immense scope for the camera!

"Schools" class 4–4–0 No.931 *King's Wimbledon* coated in war-time filth working the Newcastle to Southampton Forces Leave train, passing over Goring troughs on the Great Western in August 1945. By this time the engine has acquired a multiple-jet blastpipe and double chimney.

Ex S.E.C.R. "L" class 4–4–0 No.31778, built in 1914 by Borsigs in Berlin is seen here in mixed company at Eastleigh shed in 1952.

On show at Brighton shed, 5th October 1952, ex L.B.S.C. 1.3 4–4–2T No. 32091 (withdrawn from service) followed by K class 2–6–0 and 4–4–0 "School" class locos. Actually 32091 was the last of the class to be built, and, curiously, the last to be withdrawn.

"In Disgrace." One of the "River" class 2–6–4T's No.804 *River Tamar* (with another just behind) at Reading S.R. Sheds being steamed for removal to shops for conversion to the U class 2–6–0 tender engines, after the Sevenoaks derailment of August 1927. This photograph was taken in November of that year. The building behind is the now demolished East Main Box of the Great Western Railway at Reading.

One of the "old faithfuls" returning to duty on the removal of the "River Tanks" in the Autumn of 1927. Ex S.E.C.R. F.1 class 4–4–0 No.9 (built in 1833 and scrapped in 1932) is seen here at Reading S.R.Shed yard. This engine had been a regular performer on the branch for many long years (see photo plate on page 11). Photo taken November 1927.

Ex.S.E.&.C.R. "D" class 4–4–0 No.31586, working the 12.5pm. Reading to Tonbridge train, enters Wokingham station. The Nationalisation renumbering is on the buffer-beam, and the loco has no smokebox plate. This shows a typical S.E.C.R. train with the three-coach "birdcage" set. 10th September 1952.

Once again the Birkenhead-Dover train, but in much later years and labelled "Birkenhead-Margate". This time it is headed by U class 2–6–0 No.31804, which is one of the "River Tanks" rebuilt. Photo taken on the New Incline, a connecting line built during the last war between the Great Western and Southern Railways, in place of the original with steep gradients. Note the Great Western train in background, being the 12.30 pm ex Paddington to Weymouth running on the down main. Date 1949.

The Birkenhead to Dover through train in 1925 headed by S.E.C.R. F.1 class 4–4–0 No.9 (see plate on page 9) passes Earley station. Note the S.E.C.R. bracket signal still working. There was a gale blowing at the time, hence the exhaust keeping up with the engine!

"Lord Nelson" class No.865 *Sir John Hawkins* on the down Bournemouth Belle near Hook in 1931.

"Schools" class 4–4–0 No.931 *King's Wimbledon* working the Birkenhead to Bournemouth through train, leaving Reading West station (Great Western), in 1937.

"King Arthur" class 4–6–0 No.787 (without "blinkers"), named *Sir Menadeuke*, with a train of ancient and modern L.S.W.R. stock, works an up Bournemouth fast near Basingstoke in 1926.

Lord Anson No.861 at work, leaving Dover on the "Golden Arrow" in 1933.

L.M.S. built Diesel-Electric Loco. No. 10,000 at work on the Southern on the down Bournemouth Belle, approaching Hook in 1953. This was one of the original "twins" built by the L.M.S. in 1947 and represented our first main-line express Co-Co 1600 h.p. diesels, which are now scrapped.

"Lord Nelson" class 4–6–0 No.859 *Lord Hood* on an up Boat train passing through the Warren between Folkestone and Dover in 1931.

L.N.E.R. V.2 class 2–6–2 No.60893 on loan to the Southern Region, working the down Bournemouth Belle, approaches Basingstoke in 1953.

Ex S.E.C.R. F.1 class 4–4–0 No.117 (built 1895 and scrapped in 1936) working an Eastbourne Excursion train from Reading. It is seen here passing Earley station in 1926 with a mixture of L.S.W. and S.E.C.R. stock, not forgetting the typical 6-wheeled S.E.C.R. van at head with the "bird cage" look-out.

Two views of ex L.B.S.C. D.1 class 0–4–2T No.229, originally "Dorking" (built in 1884 and scrapped in 1947), seen here at Guildford working to Horsham. The photos were taken in 1922.

S.15 class 4–6–0 No.30829 on a West of England route freight train passes Winchfield station in 1954.

"WHAT WE FIND!"
Piston valves from an N class 2–6–0 (in the background) photographed at Reading S.R.Sheds in 1949.

The famous Observation Car at tail end of the "Devon Belle", taken at the fly-over at Worting Junction near Basingstoke in 1950. (Incidentally a difficult shot to time accurately, the train occupies the WHOLE of the negative!)

Folkestone Harbour Incline Brake No. 55181. This brake was used on the Folkestone Harbour branch where the ruling gradient is 1 in 30, and it will be seen that the body has apparently been mounted on an old tender underframe. Photographed at Folkestone Junction station on 29th May 1952.

A very hasty shot when this Inspection Saloon was seen on rear of an express stopping at Basingstoke in 1956 — the coach appears to be of L.S.W.R. origin.

"Lord Nelson" class 4–6–0 No.859 *Lord Hood* on an up West of England fast comes under the fly-over at Worting Junction, near Basingstoke in 1946. The Distant signal was "on" further back around the curve, hence the driver is looking for the "Home".

H.15 class 4–6–0 No.30473 in company with a mixture of Great Western locos. in the shed yard at Reading (Great Western) in 1959.

2-NOL Electric Unit working a Waterloo -Weybridge service at Virginia Water in February 1955.

N Class 2–6–0 No.834 on an Exeter train leaving Ilfracombe on the start of the 1 in 74 to 1 in 36 grade to Mortehoe; the rise of the 1 in 74 can be seen by the angle of the station in background. Photo taken in 1926.

What we called the REAL Birkenhead-Dover through train, this time headed by "River Tank" No.801 *River Darenth* passes Palmer Park near Reading, on the climb of the 1 in 156 grade to Earley, in 1926. The driver looks almost the same man as in photo on page 11 — one wonders!

An immaculate "Lord Nelson" class 4–6–0 No.860 *Lord Hawke* on the 3 pm West of England from Waterloo in 1929.

"Merchant Navy" class 4–6–2 No. 21/C/15 *Rotterdam Lloyd* on the down Bournemouth Belle at Winchfield in 1947.

34095

Ex L.S.W.R. "700" class 0–6–0 No. 30316 on a down freight passes Southampton Central station in 1957. This engine was built in 1897 (scrapped 1962) and was the first of the class to be superheated in 1920.

Ex L.S.W.R. S.15 class 4–6–0 No. 30499 on a down West of England route freight enters Basingstoke in 1956.

"West Country" Pacific No.34095 *Brentnor* on a down Bournemouth express passing Basingstoke in 1956. The ex Great Western branch to Reading goes off just behind that house, and into a cutting.

Ex L.S.W. Adams 445 class 4–4–0 No.448 (built 1883 and scrapped in 1924) photographed whilst on station pilot duties at Guildford in 1922. Although with only two years to go and on menial duties, her condition is worthy of notice.

Ex S.E.C.R. "R" class Stirling 0–6–0T No.1070 at Reading Southern sheds in May 1931. The engine was especially "dug out" for photographic purposes that day, being one of the few representatives of the class which was never rebuilt from the Stirling features; built 1898, scrapped 1942.

Ex L.S.W. T.14 "Paddlebox" 4–6–0 No.459, as superheated by Urie, working the 5 pm West of England from Waterloo in 1929. This valuable subject was photographed at Winchfield under difficult lighting.

Ex.L.B.S.C.R. "H2" class Atlantic No.32424 *Beachy Head*, the last survivor of its class, seen here at Brighton after working an enthusiasts' Pullman Special from Victoria on 5th October 1952.

Ex S.E.C.R. "E" class 4–4–0 No.31315 leaves Reading South station on the 12.5 pm Tonbridge train. This station is now closed and the whole area a car park, and the background underbridge has been removed. In the distance can be seen the Great Western station with the (S.O.) 8 am ex Kingswear standing in the up main platform headed by a "Hall". Picture taken in 1953.

"Lord Nelson" class No.861 *Lord Anson* standing at Dover Marine, being prepared to take on a Boat train (the Golden Arrow). Picture taken 1933.

"Merchant Navy" class 4–6–2 No. 35005 *Canadian Pacific* (still with the "Southern" plate on the smoke-box door) equipped with a mechanical stoker, works the down Atlantic Coast express near the fly-over Junction at Worting near Basingstoke in 1949.

At work on a Southampton Boat Special near Fleet in 1931 is ex L.S.W. T.9 class 4–4–0 No.120, built in 1899 and now preserved in original livery. Notice the automatic signals returning to stop on the passing of the train. This is the same bridge of signals as in picture on page 54.

A trial experiment to replace the "River Tanks" for the Birkenhead-Dover through train. Here we see an ex L.S.W. L.12 4–4–0 No.431 on that train, passing Earley Station in October 1927. Note the leading coach in all these pictures of this through train.

Ex L.S.W.R. 700 class 0–6–0 No.692 (built 1897 and scrapped 1962) in original condition passes Earley station with empties for a returning Ascot Race Special, during the famous Ascot week on 18th June 1924. Notice the two four-coach block sets, plus a couple of bogie coaches and a van; quite good seating accommodation for that occasion!

S.R. built 1-Co-Co-1 Diesel-electric 1750 hp loco. No.10202 (built 1951), working the down Bournemouth Belle, passes Winchfield in 1952. This engine is now scrapped.

Another Reading branch veteran, ex S.E.C.R. B.1 class 4–4–0 No.1217, standing at Reading (S.R.) sheds in 1949, in a rather filthy state. She was scrapped in the following year.

"King Arthur" class 4–6–0 No.787 *Sir Menadeuke* heads a down Bournemouth express as it passes Cove, near Farnborough, Hants in 1929. Note the old Bournemouth line head-code with three white discs.

"King Arthur" class 4–6–0 No.783 *Sir Gillemere* on a down Bournemouth express near Basingstoke in 1929. A special feature here is the fitting of experimental smoke deflectors around the chimney before the well-known wing plates were adopted.

A Waterloo to Reading 2 BIL electric leaves Wokingham station. The Junction with the Waterloo and S.E.C.R. Redhill route can be seen just behind the level crossing gates; the station is now being modernised, but this 1952 photo shows it in almost original S.E.C.R. design.

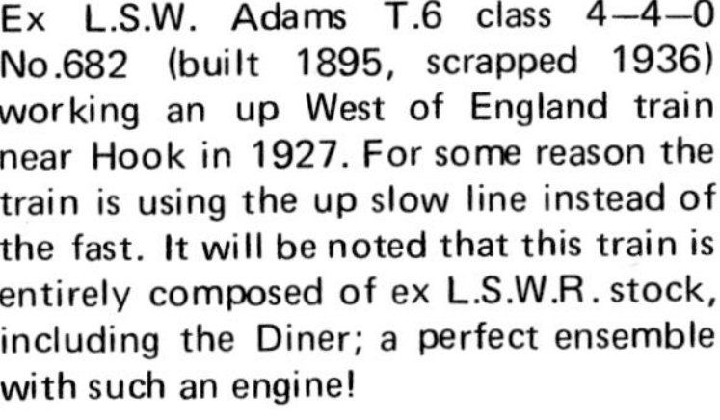

Ex L.S.W. Adams T.6 class 4–4–0 No.682 (built 1895, scrapped 1936) working an up West of England train near Hook in 1927. For some reason the train is using the up slow line instead of the fast. It will be noted that this train is entirely composed of ex L.S.W.R. stock, including the Diner; a perfect ensemble with such an engine!

Ex L.S.W.R. L.11 class 4–4–0 No.414 (built 1906 and scrapped in 1951) works a Bideford train near Barnstaple in 1925. The engine, it will be noticed, still retains the wings to the smokebox.

An ex L.S.W.R. G.6 class 0–6–0T No.258 seen standing in the shed (S.R.) yard in 1949. These engines were rarely seen at Reading before the last war when they replaced the ex S.E.C.R. Stirling 0–6–0T's on shunting work. No.258 was one of the original batch designed and built by Adams in 1894 and lasted until 1961. Note the Ministry of Supply "Austerity" 2–8–0 in background.

A Drummond T.14 4–6–0 (ex L.S.W.R.) No.443 shown as finally rebuilt by Maunsell. In their original state these engines were known as "Paddleboxes". This photograph was taken at Nine Elms in 1945 and the engine is standing on what was part of the shed, but demolished by a bomb during this last war.

B.R. class 7 4–6–2 No.70004 *William Shakespeare* leaving Folkestone Junction with an up Boat train after reversal from the Harbour branch. The tracks of the latter can be seen curving away to the right. The 0–6–0T locos which have brought the train up from the Harbour, are now at the rear, having uncoupled, and the banker is to be seen on adjoining track at the right. The photograph was taken in 1952.

Another "Lord Nelson" class 4–6–0, No.851 *Sir Francis Drake* leaving Dover on an up Boat express. The Lord Warden Hotel is in the background. Photograph taken in 1933.

B.R.Standard class 7 4–6–2 No.70004 *William Shakespeare* heads the down all Pullman Golden Arrow Boat express, near Sandling Junction in 1952.

Preparing the "Britannias" for the Boat Trains at Stewart's Lane depot. The engines are 70004 *William Shakespeare* and 70014 *Iron Duke*. The little lad sitting on the oil drum *HAD* to be included, as he really completed the composition. Photograph taken 1953.

No.30850 *Lord Nelson* himself, complete with the large chimney, working a down Bournemouth express, passes the fly-over at Worting Junction in 1957.

An unusual combination. Ex.S.E.C.R. "B.1" class 4–4–0 No.1443 (built 1898 and scrapped 1951) with L.S.W.R. "T.9" class 4–4–0 No.30708 (built 1899 and scrapped 1957). The photograph was taken in 1949 at Reading S.R. Sheds and in the background is the old Great Western East Main Box, now demolished.

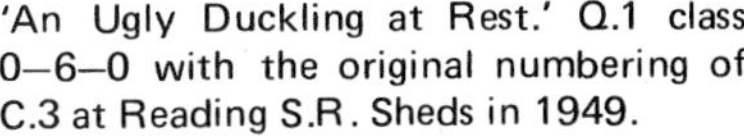
'An Ugly Duckling at Rest.' Q.1 class 0–6–0 with the original numbering of C.3 at Reading S.R. Sheds in 1949.

An ex S.E.C.R. "D" class 4–4–0 No.1728 seen here at Dover Marine. This engine was built in 1901 and withdrawn in 1953 and throughout all those years neither it nor the other members of this class were ever modified (except those rebuilt into D.1 class) and, of course, No.737 is preserved in the original splendid livery. Photograph taken June 1933.

Ex S.E.C.R. E.1 class 4–4–0 No.163 pilots an unidentified L.S.W. T.9 on a Boat express at the Bickley Junction on a miserable day in 1928.

A contrast to picture on page 15, depicts the steam days of the Reading to Waterloo service, and under L.S.W.R. guise. The engine is an ex L.S.W. M.7 No.324 and it is seen working the then 12.18 pm from Reading, passing Earley station in 1924.

"Merchant Navy" class 4–6–2 No. 21/C/18 *British India Line* on the "up" Devon Belle near Overton in 1947. The usual observation car is at the rear of the train.

Ex L.S.W. D.15 class 4–4–0 No.463 as superheated by Urie (built 1912 and scrapped 1951) working a Reading to Portsmouth through train near Southcote Junct. G.W.R. in 1933.

N class 2–6–0 No.838 climbing the 1 in 36 grade from Ilfracombe with a train for Barnstaple. The photograph was taken in 1929 near the entrance to the tunnel at Ilfracombe.

'An Ugly Duckling at Work.' Q.1 class 0–6–0 No.33018 on a Feltham to Wimbledon freight, via Chertsey. The photograph was taken at Virginia Water on a very cold and frosty morning in February 1955.

Here we see ex L.S.W. L.11 class 4–4–0 No.172 (built 1904, scrapped 1952) on an empty stock train for Southampton passing the fly-over at Worting Junct. Basingstoke in 1931. It will be noticed that the engine still retains the original smoke-box wings. The up Bournemouth line is seen on the higher level behind the train, eventually crossing the girder bridge over the West of England line.

"King Arthur" class 4–6–0 No.785 *Sir Mador de la Porte* on a Birkenhead to Bournemouth through train. The photograph was taken in 1931 as the train enters the Basingstoke branch just beyond Southcote Junction, Reading.

Again the Birkenhead to Bournemouth through train, but this time passing Tilehurst station (Great Western) headed by a L.S.W. T.9 class 4–4–0 No.301, as superheated by Urie. The engine was built in 1900 and scrapped in 1959. The first six coaches are L.S.W. stock (including the Diner) and the rest Great Western. The yard in the foreground is now a car park, and that ugly telegraph pole by the signal at the rear (a menace to all photographers) has only recently been removed. Photo taken in 1924.

A beautifully prepared "Schools" class 4–4–0 No.902 *Wellington* (not long out of the shops) seen here at Reading S.R. shed. This engine had been especially cleaned for an exhibition at Crowthorne station, presumably for inspection by the pupils and staff of Wellington College, after which school the engine is named. The smoke screen in background is from another engine. Photograph taken at the end of May 1930.

An interesting photograph showing a 'stopper' headed by an ex L.S.W.R. "Jubilee" class 0–4–2 No.617 (built in 1892 and scrapped in 1938). The location is near Southcote Junction (Great Western) near Reading. Observe the duty number of the head disc above the left-hand buffer.

S.E.C.R. "E.1" class 4–4–0 No.1507 standing in the yard at Dover sheds in 1933. This engine is one of the famous rebuilds from original "E" class S.E.&. C.R. engines.

A rare visitor to the Reading Southern station. One of the S.R.Co-Co Electric locomotives No.20001 on a special train of L.M.S. stock leaving Reading (S.R.). This 1951 photograph was taken by the "Spur Box" & Reading Gas Works, and the new incline to the Great Western can be seen on the right.

Ex L.S.W. Adams 460 class 4–4–0 No.0468 (numbered then in the duplicate list) seen at Barnstaple shed in 1926. This engine was built in 1884 and lasted until 1928. Note the square cab windows.

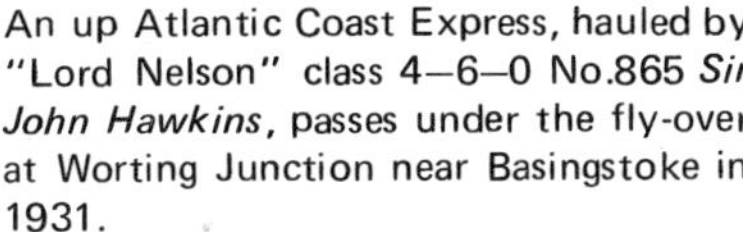
An up Atlantic Coast Express, hauled by "Lord Nelson" class 4–6–0 No.865 *Sir John Hawkins*, passes under the fly-over at Worting Junction near Basingstoke in 1931.

Ex L.B.S.C. 4–6–4T was rebuilt as a 4–6–0 tender engine and named "Stroudley". Here it bears part of its original number and is seen as 32332. The photograph was taken at Winchfield on a Basingstoke semi-fast from Waterloo in 1952.

Good for a number of years yet. Just after an overhaul and a re-paint and lined in the B.R. black livery, is an ex L.S.W.R. T.9 4–4–0 No.30287 seen here at Eastleigh in 1950. This engine was finally scrapped in 1961.

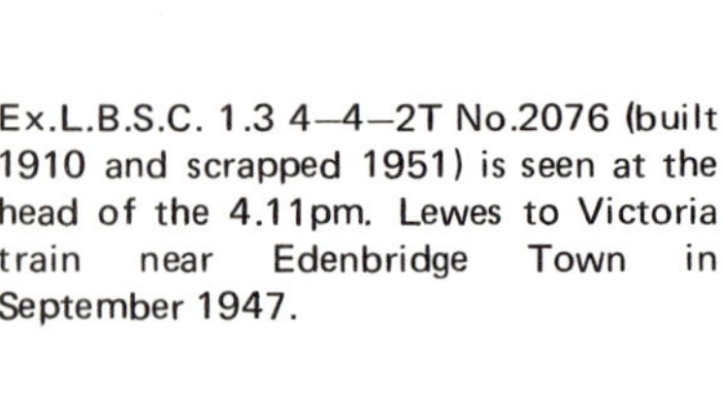

Ex.L.B.S.C. 1.3 4–4–2T No.2076 (built 1910 and scrapped 1951) is seen at the head of the 4.11pm. Lewes to Victoria train near Edenbridge Town in September 1947.

"Battle of Britain" Pacific No.34061 *73 Squadron* on a down Bournemouth express passing under a typical signal bridge of the L.S.W.R. The low pressure pneumatic signals have now, alas, been replaced by colour lights. Photo taken at Hook in 1950.

It was somewhat rare to see a Southern engine bearing the train identification numbers of the Great Western origin, but they can be seen on a "U" class 2–6–0 No.1633 heading a Birmingham to Bournemouth through train nearing Reading West station in 1935.

Ex L.S.W.R. H.16 4–6–2T No.30517 on an enthusiasts' Special passing Earley station in 1954. Compare this with the picture of No.520 taken 30 years earlier. The first coach appears to be one of the batch built for Continental services on the S.E.C.R. around 1921 and has flat sides.
Other picture on page 58.

"Merchant Navy" class 4–6–2 No.21/C/9 *Shaw Savill* on the 1 pm ex Waterloo to Plymouth express, near the station at Winchfield in 1947.

Ex L.S.W. Adams X.2. class 4–4–0 No.577 (built 1890, scrapped 1933), working a Reading-Basingstoke-Salisbury stopper, leaves Reading West station on the Great Western in 1931.

L.S.W.R. class S.15 4–6–0 No.499 in original condition at Basingstoke in 1922. Compare the appearance of this engine with the picture of her on page 25 of later years.

Ex L.S.W.R. H.16 class 4–6–2T No.520 working a Reading to Feltham afternoon freight. Seen here passing Earley station in 1924. Notice the S.E.C.R. bracket signal. The immaculate condition of this engine on freight duty is worth mentioning, but quite usual in those days!

Lynton & Barnstaple 2–6–2T No.760 *Exe* on a train at Barnstaple in June 1925. *Exe* was built by Manning Wardle of Leeds in 1897. The whole line was closed and the effects sold in September 1935.

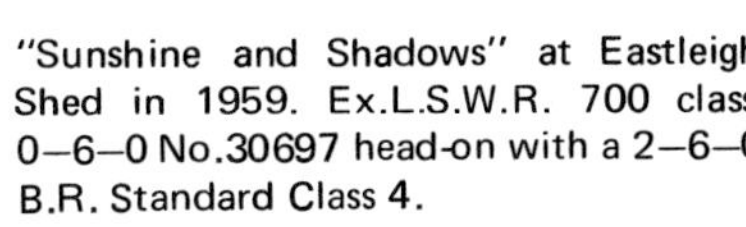

"Sunshine and Shadows" at Eastleigh Shed in 1959. Ex.L.S.W.R. 700 class 0–6–0 No.30697 head-on with a 2–6–0 B.R. Standard Class 4.

"Schools" class 4–4–0 No. 30902 *Wellington* on a down West of England fast express, near Basingstoke during 1959. Note the addition of the A.W.S. equipment.

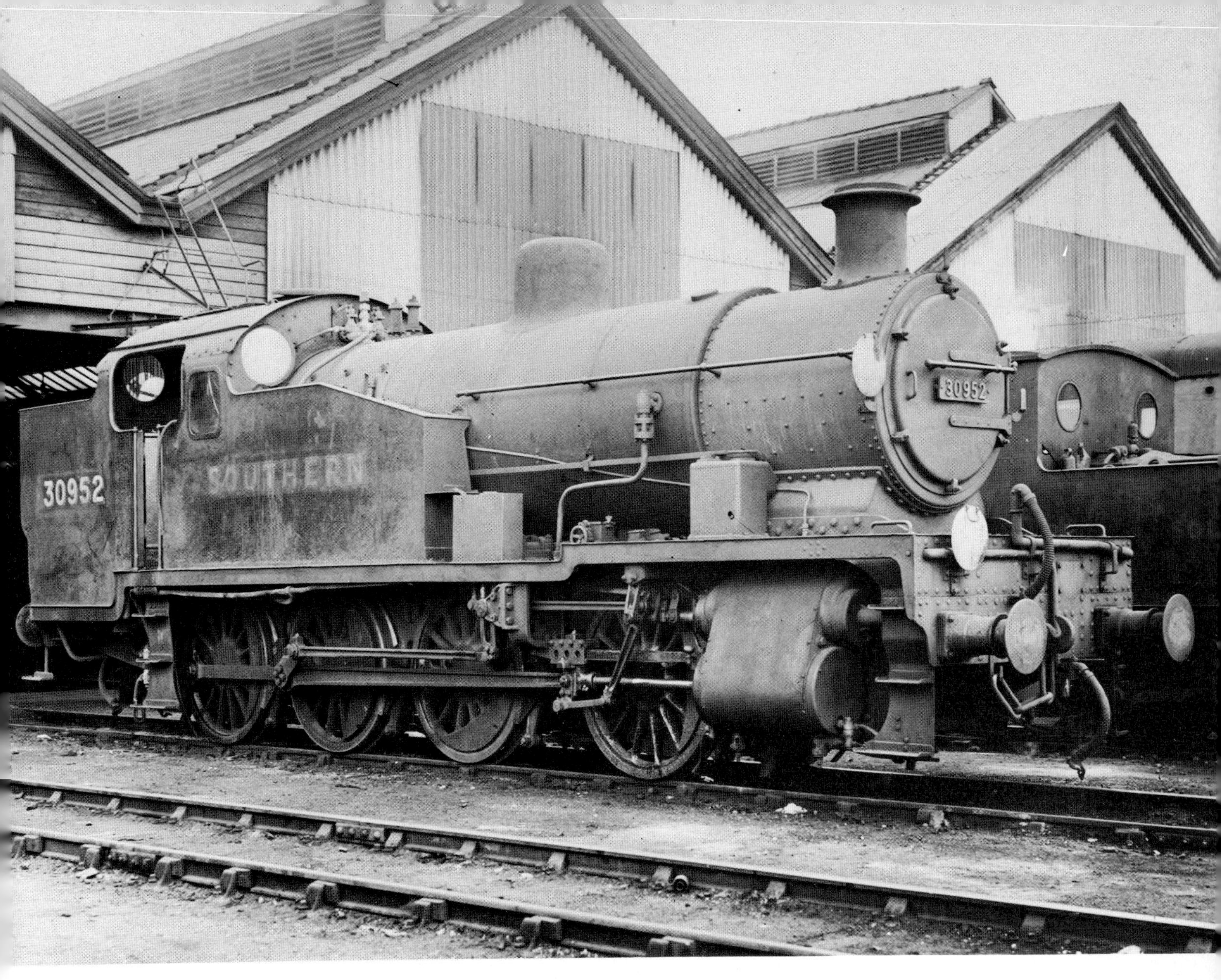

A rather rare subject to find, a Z class 0–8–0T No.30952 seen at Eastleigh sheds in 1950. There were only eight members of this 3-cylinder class shunting engines.

Ex L.S.W.R. S.15 class 4–6–0 No.515 on an up freight from Southampton seen here near Hook in 1926. It will be noticed that the engine is burning oil fuel (see tender tanks) owing to the coal strike during that year.

Ex L.S.W.R. Adams T.3 4–4–0 No.563 (built 1893) and ex L.B.S.C. "Terrier" No.82 *Boxhill* (built 1880) in Reading Great Western shed yard, en route to Eastleigh for full renovation in their original liveries for Clapham Museum. Date 1959.

"THREE plus ONE"
R.1 class S.E.C.R. 0–6–0T's Nos.31047, 31128, 31337, and banker at the rear 31154 at work on an up boat train, climb the Folkestone Harbour branch approaching Folkestone Junction. There the train is reversed and taken on by a main-line engine. Picture taken in 1952.

The author would like to express his sincere thanks to the Southern Railway Company and its successors, the Southern Region of British Railways, for their kind and ready assistance which has enabled him to take so many pictures over the past years, not forgetting the many valued friends he has made amongst the railwaymen, and the many enjoyable hours spent with them "on location".